BOLD KIDS

CHILDREN'S ZOOLOGY BOOK WITH INTERESTING AND INFORMATIVE FACTS

No part of this book may be reproduced or used in any way or form or by any means whether electronic or mechanical, this means that you cannot record or photocopy any material ideas or tips that are provided in this book.
Copyright 2022

All images in this book have been reproduced with the knowledge and prior consent of the artists concerned, and no responsibility is accepted by producer, publisher, or printer for any infringement of copyright or otherwise, arising from the contents of this publication.

You may be curious about hippopotamus and wonder how they survive. The first thing you must know about hippos is that they live in the water for most of their lives.

They cannot swim, but they spend most of their day in the water to stay cool from the harsh African sun. This is why hippos are also known as crocodiles. Here are some Facts about Hippos for kids.

A hippos can stay underwater for thirty minutes. This is probably the main reason why they float around by kicking off the bottom of the river. A male hippos can weigh up to 10,000 pounds.

They have one baby, which weighs between fifty and one hundred and ten pounds. Unlike most animals, hippos only have one offspring. The rest of the time, hippos are social and live in groups.

Hippos are large semi-aquatic mammals. They have a barrel-shaped body with short legs and tails, and massive heads. They have pale pink undercoats and greyish brown skin.

Their eyes are covered in a clear film. In addition, they have the ability to swim and float for up to thirty minutes. Their glistening skin helps them stay cool in warm water. They have large jaws and can weigh up to three thousand pounds.

Although hippos are often associated with water, they also live on land. They spend most of their lives in water, where they graze during the day.

In addition to this, they fight and play with other hippo species. They will even approach other hippos to mate. The most common species in the wild is the African hippopotamus. This mammal lives in South Africa, Asia, and Africa.

Hippos live in the water. Their eyes and nose are located on the top of their head. They breathe while submerged in water, but when they are not in the water, they can breathe.

They produce an oily red liquid which protects their skin and acts as a sunblock. While hippos used to live across the continent, they are now confined to specific areas of East Africa. This is not good news for the animals.

Hippos are incredibly social animals. They live in pods, sometimes as many as 20. Their pods are made up of adult males, juveniles, and young.

The males tend to dominate the group, and the females are the only species that do not have a leader. A hippo is a member of a group of the megafauna and will approach other members of the same species.

Hippos live in groups, ranging from ten to twenty animals. They can move through water by pushing their tails and hopping on the riverbed. The animals also produce an oily substance on their skin, which helps keep them cool and protects them from the sun.

While hippopotami are a social animal, they cannot swim. They prefer to live in groups. However, this doesn't prevent them from interacting with other humans.

Hippos are also very friendly. They will approach and attack people in order to eat them. In fact, a hippos' mother and her infant will even graze away from each other.

A hippopotamus has two babies a year. The infants weigh between 50 and 110 pounds. They are aggressive and can snore. They are also very protective of their young.

The mighty hippos can survive in water for more than 30 minutes. While they can't swim, they float around by kicking their tails and swimming up the river.

They usually have only one baby and weigh about fifty to 110 pounds. It's common for them to have a baby every two to three years. A female hippo can weigh up to 10,000 pounds. There is no way to tell if a hippo is pregnant.

In Africa, hippos are the most dangerous land mammal. They have few predators, but humans are the biggest threat to them. They are not endangered, but they are at risk of being killed.

The only way to protect the animals is to keep them safe. It is recommended for children to learn about the different hippo species and the facts they can relate to. There are several interesting facts about hippos for kids that will interest children.